MAGNOLIA SCHOOL

THE
WORLD ABOVE
YOUR HEAD

THE WORLD ABOVE YOUR HEAD

Animals that Live in Trees, Barns, and on Cliffs

Allan A. Swenson

David McKay Company, Inc.
New York

For Sheila, who looked up one day
and suddenly realized that an
exciting world exists where most
of us seldom think to look—
above our heads.

Illustration Credits
Department of Entomology, Oklahoma State University,
page 50; Photograph Courtesy National Audubon Society, pages
23, 32 top, 45 left; Leonard Lee Rue III, pages 2, 5, 8, 9, 13, 15,
19, 26, 32 bottom, 35, 39, 40, 44, 45 right, 47, 53, 55, 57.

Copyright © 1978 by Allan A. Swenson

Library of Congress Cataloging in Publication Data

Swenson, Allan A.
The world above your head.

SUMMARY: Describes the characteristics, life
cycles, and habitats of animals that live in
trees, cacti, cliffs, and other high places.
1. Animals—Miscellanea—Juvenile literature.
[1. Animals—Habits and behavior] I. Title.
QL49.S94   591   78-4415
ISBN 0-679-21051-2

1 2 3 4 5 6 7 8 9 10

Manufactured in the United States of America

CONTENTS

INTRODUCTION

There's a fascinating world above your head. Many creatures, large and small, live where you may never think to look—in the holes and on the branches of trees, in barns and buildings, and on the tops of cliffs and ledges. Many hide by day and emerge at night in search of food.

All these creatures above your head are part of nature's plan to preserve a natural balance between plants and animals. Some catch harmful insects and help to control rodents and other wildlife that might otherwise endanger our food supply.

Squirrels, raccoons, opossums, bats, owls, chimney swifts, woodpeckers, and hawks—all are part of the world above your head. And, many of these interesting creatures can be found in your own backyard, your school playground, or in your local park. Some even live in apartment houses, and have very social habits. Others prefer to live alone, beneath the eaves of a building, or in a nearby tree. Still others live in higher places—on cliffs and mountain tops—and you may need a pair of binoculars to help you uncover their secrets.

The swiftest birds—hawks, ospreys, and eagles—may not live next door to you, but you may catch sight of these magnificent predators when you are on field trips and outings in the country. You'll discover much more about these birds and other creatures that live in the world above your head if you know where and when to look for them. —*Allan A. Swenson*
Windrows Farm
Kennebunk, Maine

A flying squirrel

2

1

SQUIRRELS

The chattering you hear in the treetops is usually the sound of squirrels communicating with each other. These bushy-tailed tree dwellers are among the most familiar inhabitants of the world above your head.

There are several varieties of squirrels, including gray, red, fox, and flying. All are mammals and members of the rodent family. The southern flying squirrel, *Glaucomys volans* (glaw'-comb-is-vo'-lanz) is common to the eastern part of the United States, from the Great Lakes area to Mexico.

A flying squirrel doesn't actually soar through the air the same way birds do. A skin membrane that connects each of its front and rear feet acts as a parachute–glider, enabling the squirrel to "fly." The animal may leap from a tree branch into the air. But instead of dropping to a lower branch, it soars, banks, and then twists and turns as it approaches its landing spot. The flying squirrel's tail acts as a rudder to guide its flight, which may be as long as 120 feet. As it prepares to land, it flips itself to an upright position, thus reducing its speed.

Flying squirrels dine on berries, nuts, and seeds as well as on small birds and insects. Because they prefer to forage for food at night, you may not realize that these unusual members of the squirrel family live near you. Look for them in beech and maple trees after dark. In the daytime they prefer to stay at home in an abandoned woodpecker's burrow or in the hollow of a tree. Flying squirrels mate in early spring. The young, numbering from two to six, remain with their mother during spring and summer.

Fox squirrels are usually 15 to 25 inches long, and weigh up to 3 pounds. They are especially common in the eastern United States, from Pennsylvania to the Great Lakes, and in the Gulf Coast states, but sometimes they are also found as far west as Montana. They are the biggest squirrels in North America, and have gray or rust-colored fur.

Fox squirrels prefer to live in the hollows of oak, hickory, and other hardwood trees. They also make treetop nests of bark, leaves, and twigs. During the summer, their nests often look scraggly. In the fall, however, the squirrels improve their homes for the winter by adding more leaves to form a tightly matted roof and sides that protect them from severe weather.

Fox squirrels feed on tree buds and berries during the summer. In winter they dine on nuts and seeds which they have buried in the ground or stored in tree hollows. The term "squirrel away" stems from the squirrel's habit of hoarding its favorite foods for winter use.

Fox squirrels usually bear two to four young early in the spring. The females take on all the work of raising the

A red squirrel.

A gray squirrel.

babies. Because fox squirrels tend to be plump and slow, they often become meals for large owls, bobcats, foxes, and even human hunters.

Frisky red squirrels are perhaps the most agile and active of the species. Although their habit of gnawing into houses has earned them a bad name, these small, fleet-footed animals are less destructive than most people think.

Fully grown red squirrels range from 10 to 12 inches long, but weigh only 5 to 10 ounces. They live throughout the northern states and most of Canada. They are also found as far south as the Carolinas. They are sometimes called "Chickarees," a name they most likely received because of their chattering calls. Their scientific name is *Tamiasciurus hudsonicus* (tay'-me-us-sigh'-yur-us hudson'-ick-us).

You may see red squirrels scurrying about in nut-bearing trees, although they also eat berries. They often live in tree hollows, but frequently set up housekeeping inside buildings and under eaves.

House cats and hawks are two of the red squirrel's most common enemies. Fortunately, red squirrels are prolific, and two or more litters may be born each year.

Eastern gray squirrels, called *Sciurus carolinensis,* (sigh'-yur-us ka'-roll-in-en-siss) range from 15 to 20 inches long and have 10-inch tails. They thrive in fields, forests, and parks of the Eastern states, and from southern Canada to Texas. In colonial days, gray squirrels were so numerous that they did serious damage to farm crops and gardens. Today they are far less abundant and have adjusted to city and suburban living. In addition to nuts and grain, gray squirrels eat seeds, berries, twig buds, and, on occasion, small birds and their eggs. During summer and fall, gray squirrels bury the nuts they gather in the ground or in tree holes.

You'll find gray squirrels nesting in the hollows of trees or in leaf-and-twig nests on high branches. Their first litter of two to four babies is born in early spring, and a second litter is usually born during the summer. Their natural enemies include bobcats, domestic cats, hawks, owls, and foxes.

2

OWLS

American Indians called owls "watchers-in-the-night" because these birds of prey search for food only after sundown. In the daytime owls usually sleep in the holes of trees or tall cactus plants or on the rafters of dark buildings and other secluded places.

Owls have especially keen hearing which helps them to locate the movement of mice and other prey, even on the darkest nights. Their eyesight is keen, too. Because their eyes are fixed in bony sockets, they must turn their heads to scan their domain. Although they are unable to focus on a moving object, they can swivel their heads 270 degrees—which explains why an owl's head appears to be out of joint when the bird is looking over its shoulder.

Screech owls are odd-looking little birds with heads that seem too big for their bodies. They abound in forests, orchards, and woodland areas. Although they prefer to live in abandoned woodpecker holes, they sometimes nest in man-made wooden boxes, placed high in the trees.

This species is common throughout the United States

A screech owl.

and Southern Canada. Its call, "whoo—whoo—whoo—whoo—whoo," is most often heard just before dawn. The hoots start on high notes and become progressively lower.

The bird, usually gray or brick red, is about 8 to 10 inches long, with a wingspread as wide as 2 feet. Its scientific name is *Otus asio* (o'-tuss a-she'-o), and it is also known as the gray or shivering owl. Unlike many

8

migratory birds, it usually winters where it lives, deep inside the hollow of a tree.

After the screech owls' eggs hatch in spring, the parents catch mice, moths, grasshoppers, frogs, and small snakes to feed their owlets. The babies open their eyes 2 weeks after hatching.

Elf owls, the smallest of the species, are found in the desert regions of the Southwest. They dine on insects,

A barn owl with a meadow mouse.

lizards, toads, small snakes, and desert mice. Only 6 inches long, these little birds live in holes near the tops of tall cactus plants.

Barn owls, about 18 inches long, have dark eyes and white, heart-shaped faces ringed with tan. They are sometimes called monkey owls because their faces resemble those of monkeys. These long-legged birds have white underfeathers, and their wings and backs are golden brown streaked with gray. They can be found throughout the United States and in parts of Central and South America.

Barred owls, about the same size as barn owls, have distinctive barred-feather patterns of dark and light bands. Their call is unusual, too. It sounds like "who cooks for you." This species lives in hollow trees in the swamps and forests of North America. Their diet is similar to that of other kinds of owls, but also includes freshwater fish.

The great horned owl is also called the big hoot owl. Its powerful beak and claws make it one of the strongest birds of prey in North America. It is 22 inches long, with a wingspread that often exceeds 3 feet. Its tufted ear feathers resemble horns.

Great horned owls usually are found in forests. However, they seem equally at home in the suburbs. Their large size and great strength enable them to catch larger prey, including mice, rats, house cats, pigeons, muskrats, and even smaller owls. Two of these owls may eat as many as 8,000 mice a year, thus helping to prevent their prey from destroying grain and garden crops.

Owls cannot easily digest all parts of their prey. The

undigested parts, regurgitated by the owls, are called "owl pellets." You may find these pellets scattered beneath a tree in which an owl nests.

When the owls' food supply is scarce, nature has a way of helping reduce the owl population. Owls begin to incubate their eggs as soon as they are laid, unlike other birds that fill their nests with eggs before incubating them. This means that owls hatch progressively. Baby owls may be several days apart in age. The oldest eat first, become stronger, and grow more quickly. If there is not enough food in the parents' hunting area, most baby owls won't survive.

If you look for owls at night, use a strong flashlight. You probably won't hear an owl when it swoops to catch its prey because its fluffy feathers muffle its flight. If you shine your flashlight on the tops of trees where owls might live, the birds will usually remain motionless, hoping you won't see them on their lofty perches. If you search for owls in the predawn darkness during spring and early summer, you may be rewarded with the sight of several baby owls perched on a tree limb.

3

SWALLOWS, SWIFTS, AND MARTINS

Swallows and swifts are well named. Swallows and their purple martin cousins, catch a wide variety of insects while they swoop through the air. Swifts also dart and dive as they snare insect meals while aloft.

In the world of birds swallows, swifts, and martins are perhaps the most efficient insect catchers. Their wide bills are ideal for gathering insects in flight. They prefer to live in communities, on rafters or porches, in barns, on the sides of cliffs, and even in ready-made bird houses and on the roofs of apartment buildings.

Perhaps the hungriest and busiest insect-catching birds are purple martins. These graceful, purple-feathered birds usually make their homes in abandoned woodpecker holes, but they are also attracted to bird houses with many individual compartments. If you provide them with multiroom houses, which you can build from designs available from the Audubon Society or your

Male and female purple martins.

local garden center, you will be rewarded with the aerial acrobatic shows the martins stage all summer long.

Purple martins, our largest native swallows, measure 8 inches from head to tail. Males have lustrous blue-black feathers. Female are blue-black, with gray bellies and patches of gray on their backs.

Each martin may catch hundreds of insects every day for itself and its young. They build nests of straw and twigs in the houses people have erected on tall posts. These birds prefer a great deal of space around their homes, because as they return from their bug-catching trips, they fly directly into the openings of their own apartments. The birds never seem to pause or hesitate, but whisk right through the entrances.

During the summer, purple martins can be found from central Canada to Mexico. After raising their young, they fly thousands of miles each fall to their winter feeding grounds in Brazil.

Other types of swallows vary in size, but all are smaller than the purple martins. Unlike most birds that nest in pairs, swallows are more community-minded, and they like to live together in large colonies in man-made, multiroom birdhouses.

Cliff swallows are skilled engineers. They attach their gourd-shaped, mud nests, with side entrances, to the walls of buildings or cliffs. You may locate dozens, or even hundreds, of pairs of cliff swallows living in one small area from which they commute daily to the places where they catch insects.

The cliff swallow has a buff colored back, which is easily seen when the bird is in flight. It can also be identified by the creamy white spot on its forehead and its short, almost square tail. Cliff swallows can also be identified by the fringe on their bills, a device that helps them to snare their food in flight. Also called an eave or mud swallow, the bird's scientific name is *Petrochelidon pyrrhonota* (peh-tro'-kell-eh-don pie-row-not'-a). A powerful flyer, it can soar for hours, while devouring large amounts of insects.

Cliff and other swallows are welcomed by gardeners and farmers because they help to control insects that are harmful to crops and plants.

The barn swallow, *Hirundo rustica* (her-un'-doe rus'-tih-ka), builds mud-and-leaf nests on the rafters of barns, under the eaves of buildings, and in other sheltered spots. They can be found from Alaska to Maine, and from Canada to Mexico. You may see them near ponds and

A barn swallow on its nest.

streams, where they gather mud for these nests and catch insects. Barn swallows have sharply forked tails, cinnamon colored breast feathers and foreheads, and bluish black plumage on their heads, backs, and wings.

These birds originally nested in tree hollows and holes in cliffs. But, with the coming of settlers to North America, the swallows discovered that barns and houses were ideal places in which to make their nests.

Barn swallows have little fear of people, and you may be able to examine one of their nests on the rafter of a porch or a garage. They build their cup-shaped nests with layers of mud pellets, separated by dry grasses, and line them with soft feathers.

All swallows return each year to the nesting sites of their parents. During their migrations, you may see flying flocks of swallows numbering in the thousands, or you may discover them roosting on telephone poles and wires.

Swifts also live on insects, which they eat while on the wing. These birds have narrow bodies, long, slender wings, and short tails.

Chimney swifts, or American swifts, are known as *Chaetura pelagica* (key-tur'-ah peh'-lah-jik-ah), and are common throughout the eastern and central United States. They arrive in North America in May from their winter feeding grounds in the Amazon River basin of South America. In the summer they often gather in groups, looking for food. As dusk approaches, hundreds may assemble at a favorite chimney roost. They usually fly in a wide circle for awhile, then they suddenly begin flying in one direction. Bird watchers call this, "the dance of the chimney swifts." When the birds approach a chimney, one by one they fold their wings and drop into the chimney opening. Once inside, they cling to the chimney's sooty walls with their sharp claws and brace themselves with stubby tails. If you could peer down a chimney, you might see many layers of swifts clustered along its walls.

Swifts roost together, but they prefer to nest in pairs—one pair per chimney. They affix their twiggy nest to the chimney wall near the top. After laying eggs and raising their young, swifts gather together in late summer for their southbound flight. Alerted by a hidden signal, they take to the air and begin their long flight to South America.

4

SPIDERS

There are thousands of different kinds of spiders in the world. Many are so tiny they are hard to see. Others, such as the hairy tarantula of the Southwest, may grow up to several inches in diameter.

The only really dangerous spider in the United States is the black widow. It has a design shaped like an hour glass on its black abdomen. Fortunately, the black widow avoids people whenever possible.

Many people think spiders are insects, but that's not so. They are *arachnids* (a-rack'-nidz), relatives of horse-shoe crabs and scorpions. When you look closely at a spider, you'll see why it is different from an insect. A spider has eight walking legs; an insect only has six legs.

Unlike spiders, insects usually grow to adulthood in distinctly different phases. Their eggs hatch into larvae, or caterpillars. These grow to full size, then form *pupal* cases from which they emerge and soon develop into their adult forms. When female spiders lay their eggs, they spin an egg sac of silky strands around each egg. Shortly after the young spiders have hatched and shed their skins, they look like miniature adult spiders.

Most spiders have two body segments joined by a narrow stalk. They have fanglike mouth parts, called *chilicerae,* (chill-ee'-ser-ai), connected to glands containing the poison that paralyzes their prey. Spiders also have feelers, or *pedipalps.* If you could examine the end of a spider's abdomen, you would see six tiny, fingerlike projections, called *spinnerets.* These are the spider's silk-making devices. From them, a spider emits a liquid which dries into the silky strands that form a web.

Once a web is complete, you'll usually find its owner in the center or on one side of it. When an insect becomes entangled in the web, the spider quickly spins more strands around its struggling victim. It then injects poison through its fangs into the insect's body, and sucks out the juices.

If you search for spiders, you'll find that some species build large, elaborate webs, while others make webs consisting of just a few strands. Still others build no webs; they stalk their insect prey, paralyze it, and then suck the juices from their victim.

Although many people dislike spiders, they are valuable allies that help to preserve the balance of nature. They eat many destructive insects, and their web threads are used to make the cross hairs in telescopes.

The most easily found spiders are the orb-weavers. Their intricate, wheel-shaped webs range from 6 to 15 inches in diameter. Young orb spiders often spin new webs every day, but the adults usually build new webs only when their old ones are destroyed. The best time to

A typical garden spider web.

A common garden spider.

watch these creatures is at dusk, when they fashion their webs.

One kind of orb-weaver is the *Leucage venusta* (lew'-kej ve-nust'-a). Its green and silver body is marked with gold. This spider prefers to spin its webs on shrubs and trees.

The common garden spider is called *Argiope aurantia* (ar'-ju-up o'-ran-chee-ah). The female is black, with yellow or orange spots on its back and abdomen. The male is yellowish brown, with a brown band across the middle of its body and a zigzag band of white on its sides.

If you see a spider web in the ceiling corner of a room, its maker is probably the common house spider. Its scientific name is *Theridion tepidariorum* (ther-id'-ee-on teh-ped-daree-or'-um). Its back legs contain "combs," with which it twists its threads around flies or other insects that trespass on its web.

Jumping spiders, usually quite small, leap about on fences, plants, and the sides of buildings. These spiders don't spin webs. Instead, they stalk their prey, leap upon it, inject their paralyzing poison into the victim, and suck out its juices.

When building a web, a spider usually ejects two lines of silk, then adds the web's framework. Spiders make several types of silk. One kind is made for the main strands of a web; another is used for connecting the main strands with the other, more delicate strands of the web.

If you pull on a piece of spider's web, you'll find that it may stretch half again as long before it breaks. This elasticity helps keep the web from being broken by a fast-flying insect, since it absorbs the impact. The most fragile strands in spider webs are only one-millionth-of-an-inch thick, yet they are strong enough to catch a moth or large fly. The sticky, gluelike substance on the interwoven strands serves as a snare for the victim.

Most spiders have poor eyesight, but they respond quickly to the movements and sounds of insects arriving in their webs. Some spiders hide at the edge of their webs, then swiftly drop on a silken strand and secure their prey in a matter of seconds.

Have you ever seen thin strands or fluffs of gossamer silk floating in the air? These are dragline silks made by spiders. When winter approaches, they climb through shrubs and trees, attached to the silken threads they emit. Winds pick up these feather-light strands and sometimes carry them many miles away.

Some spiders build hidden nests in shrubs and other plants. They use their silk threads to bend and fold leaf edges together so they can hide within and wait for their prey. Aside from a few species of insects, spiders are the only animals that actually construct traps to catch their meals.

5

OPOSSUMS

Although the opossum is slow and seemingly defense-
less, nature has provided it with a unique ability to con-
fuse its enemies. When attacked, it plays "dead," and
lies with its mouth slightly open and its eyes staring
blankly.

The opossum is sometimes called a polecat. Its scientific name is *Didelphis virginiana* (dye'-del-fiss ver-jin-
ee-an'-ah). It is about the size of a house cat, and is
usually seen in trees. It has coarse, gray fur, a hairless
tail, short legs, and a long nose. It is 15 to 20 inches in
length, with a 10- to 14-inch tail, and it often weighs as
much as 12 pounds. Its tail is *prehensile,* which means
that the opossum can wrap it around a branch or small
limb. The animal also has toes that can grasp the bark of
a tree.

Although originally native to Virginia, opossums are
found throughout most of North America and parts of
southern Canada.

Many opossums are born each year. Some survive,

while others die or become part of the natural food chain for other animals. Bobcats, foxes, mountain lions, hawks, owls, and eagles are among the species that prey upon opossums.

In one special way, opossums are unique among the animals in North America. The females raise their young in pouches, the same way kangaroos do. This type of animal is called a *marsupial* (mar-soup'-ee-al).

When the opossums' young are born, they are very tiny; more than a dozen newborn opossums can fit into a single teaspoon. The babies are so underdeveloped that the mother must carry them in a pouch on her abdomen. The blind, deaf, and hairless young animals have rela-

Baby opossums ride on their mother's back.

tively strong forelegs and sharp claws. After birth, they struggle through their mother's belly fur until they find her pouch where they nurse. If any of the young are unable to find a nipple on which to nurse for the next eight weeks, they die. Usually, there are more babies born than there are nipples inside the mother's pouch. Litters may number fifteen to twenty-five, but a mother opossum usually has only nine to fifteen nursing nipples.

After nursing for 8 to 9 weeks, baby opossums are about the size of grown mice. They often climb on their mother's back for a ride on the ground or along tree limbs. By the time the young are 5 months old, they begin exploring on their own. Their diet, like that of many other mammals, is *omnivorous,* which means they eat both vegetation and meat, including berries, fruit, grains, seeds, insects, mice, and snakes.

Opossums sleep in their dens during the daytime. They are *nocturnal* animals, preferring the dark of night in which to search for their food. This, too, is a form of protection, since many of their predators hunt by day.

The best time to look for opossums is at dusk or dawn, when you may see a mother and her babies hanging by their tails from the branches of trees. Or you may spot an opossum ambling around your home or campground in search of food early in the morning.

6

WOODPECKERS

If you hear a tap-tap-tapping sound on a tree, you may catch sight of a woodpecker. Even the smallest woodpecker can make surprisingly loud noises, especially if the tree in which it is pecking for its meal is old and dry.

There are many species of woodpeckers that spend much of their lives pecking in the tops of living and dead trees. In North America, the most common kinds of woodpeckers are the flickers, sapsuckers, redheaded, and downy woodpeckers. All live on diets of worms, grubs, and insects that are found beneath tree bark.

The scientific name for redheaded woodpeckers is *Melanerpes erythrocephalus* (mel-an-er'-pess err-ith-row-sef'-a-lus). About the size of robins, these birds are easily identified by their distinctive red heads and the white patches on their tails and wings. Their backs, shoulders, wing tips, and tails are black.

The redbellied woodpecker, *Centurus carolinus* (cen-tur'-us karo-line'-us), has a black-and-white striped back, and a small red cap along the top of its head and the back of its neck.

A downy woodpecker.   *A female yellow-shafted flicker and her young.*

Downy woodpeckers are known to scientists as *Dendrocopos pubescens* (den-drah'-kuh-pus pew-bes'-enz). This sparrow-sized bird has a white back and underparts, with black-and-white wings and tail feathers. Males have small red patches behind their heads.

Flickers are among the largest and most common North American woodpeckers. Their scientific name is *Colaptes auratus* (ko-lap'-tees or-ah'-tus). You may see them in orchards, forests, and open meadows as well as in shade trees around your home. Like many of their pecking relatives, flickers usually nest in the hollows they peck in trees or in old fence posts, but they also make their homes in highway banks or in buildings. Some nests have been spotted as low as two feet above ground, while others are more than 60 feet high.

You can identify a flicker by its large size (from 8 to 10 inches in length) and by its coloring: gold or salmon-lined wings and tail, brown back, and black breast band. When it sits or flies, you can see its white rump, which is the lower part of its back above its tail. It has a red band from side to side over the back of its grayish head. The male also has a black "mustache."

At times, you may see flickers poking into ant hills in search of brown ants and larvae. Scientists have found as many as 3,000 ants in the stomach of one bird. Flickers occasionally feast on berries, also.

When you spot a flicker gathering food in spring, watch where it flies. Then, quietly move closer to its nest. If its young have hatched, you may hear a buzzing sound as they cry for food. The parents feed them by regurgitating half-digested insects into the throats of the young.

The yellow-bellied sapsucker, or *Sphyrapicus varius* (sfy-ruh-pie'-kus var'-ee-us), is another kind of woodpecker. It is about the same size as a flicker, but has a yellow breast with black V-shaped marks along the sides. It also has black-and-white striped wing and back, and a bright red cap and throat.

Although sapsuckers eat insects, they prefer to suck the sap from living trees. If you find a symmetrical row of holes in the bark of a tree, it was probably made by the yellow-bellied sapsucker. Each little hole has slightly squared corners. The sapsucker pecks through the outer layer of bark into the *cambium* layer, or the layer containing the tree's life-giving sap. Each hole points slightly downward so that the sap will gather in the hole and the bird can easily extract it with its long tongue.

Sapsuckers particularly like the sap of poplars, maples, spruce, and pines. When these birds are plentiful, you may find that many trees have been tapped. A single tree may have a thousand or more pits in its bark.

Sapsuckers create favorable conditions for other creatures as well. Bees, ants, butterflies, hummingbirds, red squirrels, and chipmunks enjoy the sweet sap in the holes drilled by the birds. But when insects gather at the sticky holes, the sapsuckers eat the insects, too.

Sapsucking woodpeckers nest in dead trees and stumps about 14 to 40 feet above the ground. The gourd-shaped homes, nearly a foot deep, have tiny 1½-inch entrances and are lined with wood chips. Both parents take turns incubating eggs and tending their offspring.

Downy woodpeckers are usually more social than their other relatives. You may see them pecking holes in trees just outside your window. They may also eat suet if you hang it in wire feeders near your window. If you study a downy woodpecker carefully, you'll see a characteristic it shares with all woodpeckers: its first and fourth toes point backward; its second and third toes point forward. Using its sharp claws, the woodpecker is able to go up and down trees rightside up or upside down.

7

BEES AND WASPS

Most bees and many kinds of wasps are social insects that live together in large colonies. However, some types of bees and wasps prefer to live alone.

Paper wasps build nests as large as 30 inches in diameter. The wasps attach the nests to tree branches or to the eaves of buildings. Paper wasps are also sometimes called white-faced hornets or bald-faced hornets. Their scientific name is *Vespula maculata* (ves-pew′-la mack-you-la′-ta). If you annoy them or strike their hives with rocks or sticks, you may be attacked and painfully stung.

Paper wasps collect bits of weathered, grayish wood, which they chew into a pulp. They then mix the pulp with a sticky saliva to make a paperlike material for their nests—a process similar to that used in commercial paper making.

A queen paper wasp attaches the first layer of paper material to a branch or a building with her glue. The glue holds the entire weight of the completed nest and all its eventual inhabitants. After making this attachment, the queen builds many paper cells and lays an egg in each.

When the eggs hatch, the queen feeds the larvae with insects she has caught, chewed, and partially digested. She continues building more cells and laying more eggs until the larvae emerge as adult female wasps, or "workers." This process usually takes about ten days. When the first workers emerge, they take over the nest building and the feeding of the larvae, while the queen turns her full attention to egg laying.

In its early stages, the nest may consist of no more than a few dozen cells which the queen has made. As the workers continue building the nest, they add a roof which protects the growing colony from the weather. If you are able to watch a nest being built, you'll be amazed how fast the worker wasps do their job.

You may not notice a paper wasp nest in a tree until it is near completion, since its color blends into the shadows beneath the leaves and branches. You may discover that some workers are busy cleaning the nest's cells so that the queen can deposit more eggs in them. Other workers take turns cleaning cells and building new cells to enlarge the nest, while still others are busy covering the entire nest with a weatherproof paper coating.

During the spring and early summer the nest contains only the queen and the workers. In late summer, however, both male and female wasps emerge from the larvae and these wasps mate. All the female workers and the males die each year, but the queens hibernate late in the fall. They emerge in spring, and start new nests the following spring.

In winter, you may be able to find an abandoned wasps' nest for classroom study. If you cut the nest open you will see its complex living quarters—the many cells that formed the paper wasps' home.

Unlike paper wasps, mud dauber wasps live solitary lives. They usually attach their nests to porches, patios, the exposed beams of buildings, or under eaves. You often can find dauber wasps around pools and roadside ditches, where they gather the mud for their nests. The large head and thorax of the dauber wasp is connected to its abdomen by a slender waist. You can identify a mud dauber by its shiny black body and rust-colored wings.

The female dauber gathers mud in her jaws, then flies to the spot she has chosen for her nest. She mixes the mud with her own saliva, and makes the mixture into a tiny ball with her jaws. By attaching these mud pellets together, one by one, she forms a ringlike nest. Eventually, she may build a dozen nests in the same location. When each is completed, she hunts spiders, paralyzes each with her stinger and tugs several into each nest. Then she lays an egg in the nest and seals the nest end with mud. Each larva soon hatches and eats the bodies of the spiders. The larvae then enter their *pupal* stage of development in which they begin to change into adults. When this process is completed, the new adults chew their way out of their mud nests to begin their life cycles.

Honeybees that live in trees have much the same habits as the domesticated bees which are raised in hives. A single queen rules the hive and lays eggs that hatch into larvae. Worker bees, the undeveloped females, tend and feed the larvae until these mature and emerge to join the hive's work force. Males, called drones, lack stingers and

A mud-dauber wasp at the entrance to its nest. When the wasp kills an insect, it places its victim in one of the nest's chambers.

Wild honeybees swarming for a new hive.

take no part in gathering honey or caring for the hive. Their main job is to mate with the queen.

Wild honeybees make their nests in tree hollows, where branches have rotted away, or in the former homes of woodpeckers, raccoons, or other animals. Honeybee workers often fly miles each day to gather pollen from flowers and other plants. When they have collected the pollen, they store it in special areas on their legs and head home in a direct line to their nests.

Other workers remain in the hive and help to make the honey that is fed to the young and the queen. The honey is also stored for the bees' winter food supply.

Eventually, new queens emerge and mate with the males, then fly away to begin new nests. A number of workers follow each new queen. You may see a swarm of bees around a queen on the branch of a tree in your yard. Sooner or later they find a suitable hollow in a tree trunk or a crevice in a building in which to build their new home.

The carpenter bee is another common, but solitary, bee. It is much larger than the half-inch long honeybee, and is gold and black. Carpenter bees make their homes by boring holes into the sides of buildings. A female carpenter bee may make several dozen holes along the side of a building, usually high up, and protected by eaves from rain. She then lays her eggs in the holes.

There are actually thousands of different kinds of bees and wasps. Those in this chapter are the ones you're most likely to find in your own neighborhood.

8

WOOD DUCKS

Every spring, flocks of wood ducks leave their winter feeding grounds in the Southern states to wing north, where they nest and raise their young. Although smaller than their relatives, wood ducks are the most colorful of all migratory waterfowl.

The male wood duck's head is crested by glossy green feathers lined with white. Its face feathers are black and white, and its back is greenish black. The rest of its upper parts is gray or buff with black-and-white stripes. Its chest is chestnut with golden flecks. The female's plumage is grayish brown. She has a white throat, and white ring around her eyes, and a crest of greenish feathers on her head.

Wood ducks are also called "summer ducks" or "tree ducks." In the summer, you may find them nesting in Maryland and New Jersey, and from Illinois to Oregon. As fall approaches, they fly south, where they winter along the Florida Gulf Coast and as far away as Central America.

Wood ducks return each year to the same nesting spot.

A male wood duck in its nest.

Many female ducks actually come back to the same nest in which they were hatched. Others settle in neighboring trees. Drakes, or male ducks, seldom return to their native areas. Instead, they follow the female of their choice—their mate for a year—to her preferred nesting ground. A male may spend a summer with its mate in the Maine woods and the next summer with a different female in upper Michigan.

In the winter, wood ducks migrate south, where they gather together. As they feed and visit with each other, their instincts tell them that the time to mate is approaching. By midwinter, a drake and a duck will swim together, often for hours. Soon, the mating dance begins. The drake emits a high-pitched whistle and raises and lowers the feathered crest on his head. Often, he strokes the female's head with his bill, and jerks his head up and down, as if nodding to her.

Each mated pair of wood ducks may fly thousands of miles to their spring and summer destination. When they arrive, the female explores her old nest—a hole in a tree or a special nesting box put up on poles by a conservationist. As she rebuilds the nest, her mate perches on a lofty tree limb or swims in a nearby lake. After the female lays her eggs, the drake may linger awhile, but during the 4 weeks of egg incubation, he eventually flys off on his own. The female remains to hatch the eggs and raise the brood. Three days after the ducklings hatch, the mother duck encourages them to scramble out of the nest. The young ducks follow their mother in a typical "duck parade," paddling along behind her in single file. They learn to eat insects and tiny aquatic creatures in the water where they live. Eventually, their downy fluff is replaced by feathers, but they don't have brilliantly colored plumage until they reach maturity.

While the young are growing, the adult drakes are molting. Their bright feathers are replaced by duller ones. By late summer, they again shed their dull plumage and once more grow their brilliantly-hued feathers. Females molt their feathers only once a year.

By late August or early September, wood ducks begin assembling for the trip south. Unlike other types of ducks that concentrate in large flocks for their southward migration, wood ducks travel in smaller groups. Most of them spend the winter less than 1,200 miles from their summer homes.

Wood ducks have been known to live as long as 14 years. Unfortunately, many are shot by hunters each fall; but the recent creation of wildlife refuges has helped wood ducks to increase their numbers.

Whether you live in the south or the north, you can watch these colorful birds and learn more about them. Once you find a wood duck nest in the spring, mark the date on your calendar. If you visit the location on the same date the next spring, you'll probably be rewarded with the sight of a wood duck arriving on schedule to raise another family.

9

RACCOONS

Raccoons are mammals that look like masked bandits, which they are in some ways. They raid bird nests and steal the eggs, and they also have been known to rob henhouses. Also called "coons," their scientific name is *Procyon lotor* (pro-see′-on low′-tor).

Raccoons live throughout most of the United States, except for a few Rocky Mountain states. They usually grow up to 32 inches long and weigh up to 16 pounds. They have bushy, black-banded tails, and their front paws resemble tiny human hands. Their fur may be buff, brown, gray, or nearly black, depending upon where they live. Northern raccoons, for example, are usually darker and larger than those living in the south.

In some areas, especially in farm country, raccoon populations can be as high as twenty-five or more per square mile. It is more common, however, to have one or two raccoon families living in a 15- to 20-acre territory.

Raccoons prefer to make their homes in trees near water. At dusk, you may spot the animals on the ground,

A raccoon in his den.

searching for food on the banks of a lake or a stream. They often wash their food—which includes shrimp, grubs, and crayfish—in the water in which they catch them, and they sometimes carry other prey to a stream for washing before eating it. Scientists have several theories as to why raccoons do this. One is that raccoons have poor salivary glands and need the extra moisture to eat properly. Another is that some of the animals eaten by raccoons have glands which give them a disagreeable taste that can be washed away. A third theory is that the animals prefer to wash gnats, mud, and sand from their food.

Female raccoons pick one mate, and they bear three to seven babies each season. Young raccoons, born in the spring, are black-skinned with pale yellow fur. Their eyes, closed at birth, open in several weeks. Their faces are gray with black masks over their eyes, and long whiskers growing on their muzzles.

Raccoons usually make their dens in the hollows of old tree limbs or trunks, or in burrows on a cliffside. Sometimes they take over another animal's abandoned burrow in the ground or in an old stone wall. Female raccoons

Baby raccoons.

nurse their babies until they are the size of kittens and are able to follow her about in search of food.

Young raccoons enjoy meals of turtle or bird eggs, grubs, berries, grain, and nuts as well as crayfish, shrimps, and small frogs. They are strong swimmers, and have been known to dive into water to pull up mussels and to catch pollywogs and small fish. They sometimes steal eggs from duck nests along the shores of lakes and swamps. They are also fond of sweet corn. During a night's raid, they often topple dozens of corn stalks, but only nibble a few kernels from each ripening ear.

Raccoons are perhaps the most nocturnal of American mammals. In daytime, they hide in their dens. Their grayish brown coloration serves as camouflage and lets them blend into the shadows of the night.

In the northern areas of the United States, raccoons sleep in their dens most of the winter. Those that live in the southern states remain active the year round.

10

HAWKS, OSPREYS, AND EAGLES

Hawks, falcons, ospreys, and eagles are birds of prey that soar high above your head, watching carefully for movement on the ground below. If they see a mouse, a rabbit, a snake, or other creatures they take for food, they swiftly plummet downward and seize their prey. The birds are skillful hunters, with powerful beaks and strong, sharp talons. They usually make their nests in treetops and on the tops of cliffs. On occasion, you may see an osprey's massive, twig-and-branch nest on the top of a telephone pole near a waterway.

Hawks and their predator relatives are carnivorous birds, meat eaters. They have been known to kill chickens, ducks, and many kinds of songbirds. But these birds of prey play important roles in the balance of nature. Their primary diets include many animals and insects that destroy crops.

Hawks are high fliers. They use wind currents to help them soar to great heights. Some hawks are small, and

11

MONARCH BUTTERFLIES

One of the loveliest sights on a sunny spring day is a brightly colored monarch butterfly. Among all butterflies, the monarchs are well-named. The glorious colors of their wings—usually orange-brown, with black borders and white dots—and their large size combine to give them royal beauty.

Unlike most butterflies, which live their entire life in one area, monarch butterflies are wanderers that migrate the same way birds do.

Wherever you live, you probably have seen a monarch butterfly. They spend most of their time in spring and summer near woods and in sunny open areas throughout the United States. Because they are usually found around milkweed plants, they are also called "milkweed butterflies." Their scientific name is *Danaus plexippus* (Da'-nay-us plex'-ee-puss).

In early fall, hundreds of thousands of monarch butterflies begin their annual migration. They journey from 200 to 2,000 miles on their autumnal flights. They even have been observed far out at sea, and have become

49

Monarch butterflies

established on islands in the Pacific ocean from Hawaii to Java and Australia. Scientists have traced these migrations, but still do not understand why monarch butterflies, unlike others, have this migratory habit.

People who live near the Atlantic or Pacific coasts often catch sight of monarch migrations. In a given hour, a thousand or more of the species head south, fluttering over sand dunes and waves. The same instinct which spurs coastal migration warns monarch butterflies in inland areas that winter is approaching.They also take flight, heading to warmer southern climates before the fall frosts arrive.

Monarchs are well known in Pacific Grove, California, a community overlooking Monterey Bay. There, the butterflies take refuge in trees. A city ordinance, dating back to 1938, proclaims that because monarchs are an asset to the city, attracting tourists annually, it is the duty of every citizen to protect the butterflies in every possible way.

50

There is a heavy fine for anyone who harms them, and an annual parade celebrates the butterflies' arrival. Entomologists (people who study insects) report that each year as many as two million monarch butterflies spend the winter at Pacific Grove, clustering within just a few acres.

Monarch butterflies do not hibernate. Instead, they bcome semidormant (partly asleep), clinging in unmoving masses to leaves, plant stalks, and the twigs of trees.

In spring, the monarchs grow more active. Soon, they wing their way back north to mate, lay eggs, and die. Their larvae hatch from jewellike, pale green eggs, deposited beneath milkweed leaves.

Look for monarch butterflies in spring, when milkweed blossoms first appear. If you examine the underside of milkweed leaves with a magnifying glass you can witness some of the mysteries of the monarch's life. A tiny caterpillar, about one-eighth of an inch long, hatches from each egg. At maturity, the larvae are bright green caterpillars, banded with black and yellow. When fully grown, the caterpillars attach themselves, by their hind ends, to leaves. Then each forms a chrysalis—a waxy green pupa decorated with glistening spots of silver or gold.

Within 7 to 14 days, a butterfly forms inside each pupal case. In dry, warm weather, this fascinating change may occur in just a few days. When the transformation is accomplished, the monarch butterfly bursts its pupal case to emerge as a mature butterfly. As its wings dry, each monarch tests them, gently wafting them in the warm air before flying away to visit milkweed blooms.

12

SONGBIRDS

In northern areas, the music of songbirds can be heard each year in the spring, when the birds return from warmer climates. Come spring, they build their nests and begin their reproduction cycles in the same areas in which they were once hatched and raised.

Songbirds belong to the scientific class called *Aves* (ay'-veez). They are vertebrate animals, meaning they have a backbone and a skeleton. Songbirds are well designed for their activities. Their light, hollow bones help to keep their weight to a minimum for flying. Their feathers are waterproof, and provide highly effective insulation against cold. Birds that live in trees have claws that enable them to cling to branches and climb about in search of meals.

There are thousands of different species of songbirds. North America has 74 families and 736 different species.

The feeding habits of songbirds vary. Most eat insects, but some feed on seeds and grains. Others like berries and fruit.

Some birds sing sweetly, while others whistle. A few

make almost no sound at all. Flocks of some species prefer colony life in the "apartment houses" they build, while others are so timid that they try to remain hidden most of their lives. The birds described in this chapter are typical examples of those you can find and study when you explore the world above your head.

The tufted titmouse, found in the eastern portion of the United States, is a little bird with a feathered crest on its head, blue-gray back and wings, a white breast, and rust sides. Its western relative has a black crest and a white forehead. There is also a plain gray titmouse that

The male cardinal is bright red, with a black face and a pointed crest.

lives in the West, and a bridled titmouse that lives in the mountains of the Southwest. It has a white face with black markings.

You can identify the titmouse by its "pee-too pee-too" call. It searches cracks and crevices of tree bark, looking for insects and larvae. It also dines on nuts, berries, and seeds. Titmouse homes are usually found in old tree hollows deserted by woodpeckers.

Cardinals are also members of the titmouse family. The males are bright red and the females are a lighter reddish gray. They enjoy much the same diet as the tufted titmouse, and are frequent visitors to well-supplied bird feeding stations.

Orioles are insect eaters that build pouchlike nests in tall trees. The nests are attached to the ends of branches with string and other bits of cord the birds find. If you hang bits of string or yarn on the shrubs near your home, orioles may gather the material for their nests.

Baltimore orioles are bright orange and black. Their orchard oriole cousins are less colorful. Males are brick red with black tails, and the females have a greenish yellow breast.

You may catch sight of a yellow warbler in shrubs, where they build nests 3 to 8 feet above ground. You may also spot their nests of gray plant fibers and shreds of bark in the forks of low trees. The yellow warbler's grayish white eggs, spotted with brown, are hatched by the female.

House wrens nest in tree hollows or in small cavities in buildings. They prefer a home 8 to 10 feet above the ground. Their nests are lined with grass, animal hair, and

A female Baltimore oriole feeding her young.

feathers. They may lay from four to ten pinkish white eggs several times each year. These brownish-colored birds can be heard singing throughout most of the day.

Robins are common in every state. They live in forests, open land, cities, and suburbs. Red-breasted robins, with dark wings and backs, usually prefer to nest 10 to 15 feet above ground. They fashion small, bowl-shaped nests out of grass and twigs and line them with mud. Their eggs are pale, greenish blue. The birds usually raise two or three broods a year.

Robins are especially fond of worms and grubs which they pluck from the ground. You may often see a robin cock its head and then quickly grasp the tip of a worm with its beak. It will pull and tug until it has the worm tucked in its bill.

Chickadees live mostly in parks, orchards, and woods. They usually nest in tree cavities, but will also live in man-made birdhouses. The chickadee builds a nest that is several inches deep, and lines it with moss, thistledown, milkweed, and other plants and feathers. These birds lay brown, speckled eggs, and may hatch two broods each year.

Nuthatches, like chickadees, are fond of insects and seeds. These black-crested little birds scamper up and down trees, looking for food. They prefer to nest as high as 60 feet in orchards and along treelined streets. They may also use abandoned woodpecker holes for their homes. Their creamy white eggs have reddish brown spots.

Hummingbirds, only two inches long, are the smallest birds. These tiny, ruby-throated birds, with long bills and swiftly-beating wings, usually feed on the nectar of flowers. They live in trees from three to twenty feet high. Each of their cup-shaped nests, made of plant down, and bits of moss and lichen, is barely three-quarters of an inch in diameter.

The Audubon Society has chapters throughout the United States that welcome junior members. If you

A female broad-tailed hummingbird.

check into their activities, you'll find that many chapters offer "bird hikes" in your area. Chapters also conduct bird surveys during migration periods each year. They can help you to learn more about your local birds and how you can help to protect them.

If you erect a bird feeding station and keep it stocked with bird seed and water, the birds in your area may remain year-round. You'll find directions in Audubon Society pamphlets for building feeding stations and houses for wrens, warblers, nuthatches, purple martins, and other species. However, once you undertake to feed wild birds, you should continue to do so because most species of wild birds will become so dependent on you for their food that they will be unable to fend for themselves if this food supply is cut short.

61546

591   The World Above
           Your Head

           Swenson, Allan A.

DATE DUE			
FEB 21			
OCT 4			